SHADES
OF
ISLAM

SHADES
OF
ISLAM

POEMS FOR A
NEW CENTURY

RAFEY HABIB

KUBE
PUBLISHING

First published in England by Kube Publishing Ltd,
Markfield Conference Centre
Ratby Lane, Markfield,
Leicestershire LE67 9SY
United Kingdom
Tel: +44 (0) 1530 249230
Fax: +44 (0) 1530 249656
Website: www.kubepublishing.com
Email: info@kubepublishing.com

A Cataloguing-in-Publication data record is available from the
British Library.

ISBN 978-1-84774-021-2 *paperback*

Cover Design: Irfan Adrian Day
Typesetting: Nasir Cadir

DEDICATION

This book is dedicated to those Muslims, Jews and Christians who are striving to find a common path toward peace, mutual understanding and humanity.

CONTENTS

II. On Being a Muslim

III. Love?

IV. Ghazals, Sonnets and Rubaiyat

V. Political Musing

Acknowledgements

I should like to thank the following people for their expertise in commenting on my manuscript: Joe Barbarese, Harold Shweizer, Carl Ernst, Renate Holub, John Carey, Terry Eagleton, Chris Fitter, Joe Meredith, Mughni Tabassum, John Farquhar and Tyler Hoffman. I should also like to thank Chris Barrett and Elizabeth Licorish for their kind help, as well as my former students Mary Ellen Bray, Sarah Skochko, Caitlin Marmion, Alicia DeMarco and Kevin Dickinson. I am grateful to Mr. Samuel Levin for his gracious comments. The cover was designed by Irfan Adrian Day, whose artistry once again shines above my words. I would like to thank Mr. Yahya Birt for his meticulous overseeing of this project. Finally, I am indebted, as always, to my wife Yasmeen, my sons Hishaam and Hasan, my mother Siddiqua Shabnam and the memory of my father, M.A. Khader Habib.

Rafey Habib
November 2009

PREFACE BY J.T. BARBARESE

From the still limited view of our century, the twentieth century was not a period convivial to religious verse and even less to expressions of religious devotion by non-Christians. There is little or nothing in canonical Modernism to suggest that writers like Hopkins, for instance, or even a Tagore had any lasting influence on the work of the century that followed. Minor precedents such as George Herbert were safely secured as expressions of Reformation Protestantism, and major figures like Dante and Milton were salted away in New Critical practice that taught us to read by separating form from content. Other than T.S. Eliot, whose religious views were the essential complements to his political and aesthetic ones, religious poetry written in English appears (if and when it does) as the expression of outmoded, quaint sensibilities. The regnant tonality of our poetry in fact is and continues to be irony.

The irony we find in these devotionals of Rafey Habib – closer to the subtle tragedy of High Romantic poetry than the comic intellectual ironies of Modernism – befits their occasions but also reveals the divided nature of the poet and poetry itself. On the one hand this is the record of an Islamic sensibility that proclaims itself on the opening pages:

> God is the Light
> Of the Heavens and of the Earth;
> His Light is a parable, of
> A Lamp within a niche; without the lamp, a glass
> Haloed as a brilliant star, lit
> From an olive tree...
>
> – "Light: A Passage from the Qur'an"

In this dispensation, words are signs standing for other things, and those things are themselves evidence of the signature of creative intelligence on time and phenomena: Words, in this view, are

Symbols, stood in the still light;
Will not be understood
As words, signs for
Things...

The evidence of the presence of God is the *liber mundi* itself, the
world as a book autographed by an intending creator, intension
standing behind each object the way meaning stands behind each
word.

But the history of personal belief in a poet's mind is always
apocalyptic. It is continuously shaped and inevitably compromised
by personal experience, whose messiness and resistance to closure is
what makes it so seductive. A totalizing myth resolves contradiction
and anneals our confidence in the rightness of our lives, but a poet's
experience includes suffering what is contradictory and coming
to love the slipperiness of language itself. A poet's arguments are
directed not to abstractions but to the things of the world:

A woman washing her children's clothes
By the rocks of a stream,
Eyes dark, unquestioning:
The mild reflection is her only truth.
Along the shore a young man walked,
Gazing at the nearness of sea and sky,
Dust in his image ...

– "Return (to India)"

Habib's poems are thus the record of a sensibility at least thrice
exiled or removed from origins. He writes as a Muslim in a Christian
culture, as a native of Great Britain now living in the United States,
and – most alienated figure of all – a poet who is trying to live
the life of the spirit and the life of the mind at once. In poems
like "The World Does Not Hate America," he is uncompromising
in his identifying himself and his family with twentieth century
Modernism and with its explicit American expressions:

They don't hate us: that's a lie
Spewed by those who dare not travel
And a few who travel but dare not look.

Yet in poems like "Muslim Love," whose intensity is its nostalgia, he is also deeply committed to mounting an argument for the Islamic faith whose painful contradictions these poems also recount:

You think Muslims
Are repressed, that
They berate love,
That they envy you!
Let's just say: they
Have great love:
If only you knew!

In poems such as "Hymn," "Recitation" and "Prayer," Habib's verses are religious in the Islamic tradition of figures such as Saadi and Rumi and the Western tradition of Herbert, Edward Taylor, and even, if carefully read, Shelley. These were writers who resisted the tendency of ideology to solve the world and its contradictions into a happy unity and instead sought in poetry a means of sensuously investigating those contradictions. It is as if poetry had aspired to the condition of prayer itself, or prayer had taken as its goal not an escape from human feeling but to supplement it, and not to deny belief but to represent it in terms of its varied material embodiments and see the unseen through the seen, the invisible in the visible, and whatever world there may be to come in this world.

J.T. Barbarese
November 2009

PART I

RECITATION AND REVELATION

Islamic Hymn

Glorious are You, in Your
Aloneness, Your
Pale eternal splendor
Beckons, in whose
Depthless light my shadow
Burns:
Hold me in Your moving stillness;
Let my night pass in
Your day.

Sublime are You, whose
Beauty burns in all Being,
Exalting all substance
Through the far corners;
Who breathed Your light
First on the face of formlessness, and last
On the forms of Human Reason.

Serene are You, in Your
Otherness, Your
Yearning depth embraces me;
Your knowing pales before itself:
Enthroned in realmlessness,
Your wisdom's endless sea
Is adrift in my tears.

Absolute are You:
The pavilions of Night wear Your perfect Form;
From East and West Your lanterns rise:
Light upon light.

World upon world are You, Knower
Of destiny, harbinger
Of Time's still path;
Who finds me bowed
In the rhythms of fate;
Your splendor, it is in both worlds,
Your light, it fills the far corners of Being:
Here, all is You; there, all is You.

Recitation

This is the Word of God. If you recite
It before others, be sure that your voice
Is sweet and melodious: not mere noise
From an odious mouth drilled in despite.

Let the lips which shape His language of Light
Sing not just to sense, but weigh divine choice
Of syllable and word, whose divine poise
Holds the soul in its journey toward sight.

Many have fainted, hearing aloud these sounds.
Many have converted. Let me faint, too:
Let me feel His music as it resounds
In my deepest hearing, as it moves through
Sense, psyche, will and act. You who recite:
Make sound sing in my soul, till it takes flight.

Light
A Passage from the Qur'an
(Translated by Rafey Habib)

God is the Light
Of the Heavens and of the Earth;
His Light is a parable, of
A lamp within a niche; without the lamp, a glass
Haloed as a brilliant star, lit
From an olive tree, blessed;
Whose soil is neither East nor West;
Its very oil would shine forth
Though untouched by fire:
Light upon Light.
God raises to His Light whom He will;
He engenders parables for men, He
Whose knowing is beyond horizon.

His Light abides in houses, sanctified
For the adoration of His Name. There
Is He glorified, morning and evening
By those whom trade nor profit can
Divert from remembrance of God
Or steadfastness in charity and prayer;
Whose sole fear is for the Day
When heart and vision wake
In a new world
Where God rewards their deeds
Giving ever more from His Grace
For God furnishes measurelessly
Those whom He will.

– Holy Qur'an XXIV: 35-38.

Veiled Letters

Alif. Lam. Ra. These are the
Letters that will not yield. They
Stand like before and after,
The unremitting, unreturning

Face of time. Inscribed in
Uncomprehending hearts,
Unyielding faces, they are
The traces of eternity, returning

To language, overshadowing
Viewpoint and perspective
With higher harmony, notes
From sacred spheres, intoning

Veiled letters, trailing an
Invisible journey, trace
Of Otherness, whose sign
We read but cannot know.

Reading the Qur'an

Symbols, stood in the still light;
Will not be understood
As words, signs for
Things. Their wisdom shapes
The sounds they fill
From a deeper source than shrill
Persuasion. They call to deeds but
Also to silence, whose depth reaches
Beneath recitation
Through long centuries,
Exegesis, back to the voice of
 Man, treading desert sand,
Listening to voices higher than all the
Words within, around his world.
These symbols call to all the
Forces of reading: book more
Than book, whose signs
Are more than words, opening into
Worlds of self, struggle, silhouetted
Against fading of night, opening
Into red of distance;
Their voices flow, in meaning
Shivering through many realms,
Past and future,
Whose movement cannot
Be stilled; voices whose life
Might not be stifled, in schools,
Be killed in codes and ghosts of
Rules, of literal reading:
Symbols, whose sounds
Are more than meaning.

Reciting the Qur'an

Without Your Word in my heart,
I am not me; Your Word on my lips
Is not enough; it can be smudged off
By the world's kiss, alluring in softness
Of speech. Your Word in my mind,
In depths of understanding is
What creates me again, anew,
Moulds me from within, as Spirit
Shapes Form. Let me be Your
Slave, not in letter only but in soul,
In knowing. Let its flame
Burn deep within to quench all other flames,
Let its tip of brilliance be my word
Flickering at the edge of Your Word,
Blazing at the core of my heart.

Hira

For years, the darkness has draped me,
Enshrouded in the high mantle of night.
Darkness of idols, worship of Mammon,
Abuse of orphans, widows, women.
Here, from the mountain, I see a darkness
Enfolding the world. Yet now
Another darkness descends on me,
A beating of wings, shuddering,
Beating in my own breath, heart, soul:
Shadows everywhere, all shadow.
What moment is this, opening into
The very soul of time, what mode of time
Unfolding breath of
Eternity. God. Worlds above, worlds
Upon worlds. What weight of universe
Descends, spreading through me,
Breathing through my lips
A voice from so high yet so deep within
Shuddering in Angel breath: O vision
At the edge of vision, wherever I turn
My dark horizon is lit with form of Angel,
Forcing me, wherever I turn, he stands,
Blinding, colossal, power of light:
Archangel.

All the forces of mountain and desert
Cry into my heart; the black sky
Thunders in my throat:
All the sources of life, all sense, all
Reason, beauty, the sublime,
Freeze in this moment, in this cave,
All resources of language, lips, eyes, hands
Flow and freeze in this one command:
Read! Echoing inside me, pounding,
Read! My own voice. I hear
Myself, from deep within:

I cannot, I cannot read.
Again the echo, pressing louder, harder:
Read! The word, the world, bites
In my head, my frame shivering yet
Numb: I cannot read. Read!
Read in the Name of Thy Lord...
Read.

Prophet of God

Prophet of God, I am
Steeped in the things
Of sin, and wrong:
Unworthy to stand
Beside you,
Or even to sing in
Your praise.

Prophet of my heart, my
Verse is beneath you, my
Only skill, bequeathed by
Birth, perturbed dreams
Of your nights and days.

How can I come near
The cloak that wraps you,
When fear dries my throat,
When I know Who spoke
In your hearing.

How can I read, or
Understand, when I live
At the edge of His commands,
When my sins need
To feel Him forgive?

Where will I find help;
Where will I know the
Good in Self; where
Will I not be alone, if not
In the places you
Have known?

If I stand, arrayed,
Against my own desire,
For fame, prestige, wealth,
Will your shield defend
My faith, against the fire,
Against my own, lower, self?

If I come stumbling,
Across desert and
Grey seas; if I humbly call
Across the sands, will you
Reach for my hand?

Prophet of God,
Do not turn away from me;
Stay... say a prayer for me:
Unworthy to sing
In His praise.

Prophet of my heart,
My lonely art, companion
Of my unworthy
Nights and days.

Desert

Poor, my prophet, are my words:
The sole adorners of this soul.
Unsure, I thought I saw you, once
When Night had clothed me
In her holiness:
This darkness is not for me alone
But glints along the desert's edge.

Quest

In the far corners I sought you,
Of worlds which sing in our nearing;
Inside my own heart I fought you,
In sin that smiles, overbearing.

Let me see the blindness that comes
From light, the life that comes from death;
Let me know the sorrow that numbs
My body, to feel my soul's breath.

Let me hear your voice in silence;
Let your shadow blind our pale sun;
Bring me to the End of ends, whence
Our souls can show what they have done.

Let the far corners know Your Name,
Lost amid shrines, feet searching through Night;
Let your brilliance nearing blind my shame,
Let my blindness live in your Sight.

The Help

When I am weary of this life's striving,
When my faith is low in those who know me,
Do not You abandon me, my sweet God,
Let me feel you near in this fallen night.

Calm this burden in my spirit, which aches
For Your Peace, to lose itself in Your Light;
Give strength to these failing limbs, which seek rest
In a far-off place, where memory fades.

Let my wounds heal in your holy waters,
Let your Gardens blossom all around me,
Let your cleansing fountains rise before me,
And your soft Azan guide me to my peace.

Azan

Lord of the worlds, sanctify
My yearning;
Let the soul of my dream rise
To the morning of Azan;
From East and West let the minarets call;
Their music reverberate through both worlds.
Dusty echoes of a distant pilgrimage
Have crowned my hearing;
The past has resumed its tongue:
Ancient robes and words whisper on;
Forgotten martyrs gaze through memory;
Tradition has torn its silken banner:
Oppressed into myth, it soldiers in its need.

Sweet is your Name in this purity of desert;
Mirrored in the sea, echoed in the mountain;
The myth reclines under your shadow.
Night and Day kiss in your arms;
The chaos is touched with your language;
History robed in your meaning.
Far shores bewail their separation from You.

The Garden and the Fire

The gates of the One are the gates of the Other:
When open to One, they close to Another;
The Garden and the Fire are mirrors of you,
They are the two sides of our every choice;
They will echo as your eternal voice;
What we did Here will sing forever There;
The smiles we brought to bright eyes, the dark tears:
Let us speak well, my friend, for the Friend hears
From eternal skies what is whispered below;
Vast suns glare into darknesses only you know.
When this small frame falls beneath its own weight,
It will bear the weight of unseen worlds,
Galaxies that spin when all time is gone
Eyes that watch when all but darkness is done:
The Garden soft beneath white moon, shading
Us from rivers deep beneath of black Fire.

Time

The poisoned soul thinks it will live forever:
It never dreams of death.
But this life's span is but one breath
Taken by Eternity. Once gone
We can never come back, never
Heal the hurt we caused, never
Stride out from our own shadows, nor
Share the love we never showed, or
Forgive untiring moments of weakness
In friends, colleagues, our own blood.

We will wish to come back, we will beg to
Come back, for just a short
While, just long enough to
Mend our image, complete ourselves,
Make whole what we should have been.

But all the voices will answer
From the darkness, the depths of
Realms beyond time: your time is gone
Forever, your image cast forever: all
The yearning of a thousand lives
Will not bring you to the life
You lost. You will not walk here again,
Hand in hand, in gardens, laughing, beneath
Purple skies, looking on moonlit seas.
You will not breathe again
The precious air of Time.

Journey

We are undeserving of grace.

Turning, always turning
    Away.

We pretend to seek His Face.

Yearning, only yearning for
    Ours.

If judgment ever comes our
    Way

We will stand, on that shore,
    Accused

By children we waved away,
    Refused.

We came, unknowing, into trial,
    Thrown

We lived, unloving, unwilling to
    Choose

We go, unsmiling, far from His
    Throne.

Peace

My peace
Is the inward journey of an outspoken dream,
Backward, source-seeking,
On broken wings
To the cavern where red oceans roll
Into stillness

Lost contentment of old idioms,
Grandiloquent, blind:
I hear myself behind
The noisy contract of words
Language's opaque religion
Has sheltered loss:
Where is God beyond this
Ruined thought?

My peace
Is the futile march of an old wisdom
Which has craved the tears of experience
Whose goal is a backward glance
Over drying possibility.

Mosque

Here, within your white, white walls
I can stand
Alone with the Alone;
Away from the whispers of the world
That bleed in my own heart;
Away from fleeting and fancy,
From torment that thirsts
In my own soul.

I have felt You, near the rivers of my heart,
As if on the verge of a great promising.
I have sought You, bitterly, in broken lives
Of people twisted over by the world's disasters;
I have not heard Your voice, even faintly,
In the loud ramblings of imams who explain
Your justice as if it were a trite thing.
I know You are not trite or easy:
The path to You is always long;
I know I am never fit for Your presence,
I am forever beneath Your language,
I am unworthy of Your paradise;
I am not fit to fall before You.

But when
O when will You hear
The voices raised of those
Who have erased their lives in Your service,
As if on the verge of an eternal reckoning;
Who have killed their ambition
Brought their lust to kneel
Who have murdered their passion
In the coldest of blood-feuds.
When will You hear the cry of
Those who have died for You?

Cancer Cell

She waits, in caverns, tunnels,
    whose darknesses
    turn, twist

Like ancient Christians burning
    breaking
    bread in catacombs,
    waiting
    for a world to end.

She is the straining
    of faith which
    breaks the shield of empire
    chance which

Lies between earth and
    your lying heavens.

They spy on her
    with technology
    cameras, hopes

They give you lying scope
    the gentle nurse
    who takes your pulse
    smiling anesthesia

Life will go on forever, dreaming
    back in your own bed
    wife's hand, climbing children
    colleagues, parties, Sunday school

Your cycle of empire, excreting
    the foreign, feminine, savage, lawless
    cells of terror, aimless

As your stomach churns the world's
      resources, burgers, gas
      pizzas, wings, gas

You will not learn the lesson of
      the sun, glaring through her torn veil
      or of rising water, drowning appetite

You must take and take, devour, rape,
      as if heaven could not end
      as if she could sleep forever
      but she waits

You yourself will let her in
      within your own blood, citadel
      polluted, sickness in your very stomach
      ancient sack: she will multiply into hordes, flooding in

An empire falling, only broken columns, bones
      whose only cure is burning
      alive.

Tsunami I

Tsunami,
I have watched, on your silver-tipped horizon, from high stories of
hotels
The relentless whisper of your surge:
The white line rolling toward the shore,
Toward the fisherman's house, the child dreaming on rocks,
The factory worker's kitchen, the villager's corrugated walls.

Some say the name of God shone from the sea,
Shaped by illiterate waves; some say His name
Lay frowning at the ocean floor, buckling the mighty plates of earth,
Moving together vast alien worlds, like night scraping against day:
A fathomless momentum, knowing no human end.
Divine vengeance, divine sign: a warning (they say):
But here destiny and fate lie confused, merging,
Like sea and sky, no pattern emerging
Of good or evil, past or present, history or prophecy:
Merely loss, irredeemable, absolute.

Now I know,
All of life I have been hearing you:
In my own breast, in the pulsing of my own blood.
And now, fixed in fear, I watch: your waving black expanse always
Approaching, always receding into silence before
Exploding into white roar shocking the whole horizon
Into black sky of water, towering in speed, rolling
Immensity, unfolding onto land its fearsome depth...

No mountain, I know, nor hill
Shall elude your fluid paths;
All the peaks of aspiration
Will melt into you:
All things, human, non-human, all distinction done,
All will become you
In one bland and endless quiddity.
One day, I know, you will come for me,
Tsunami.

Tsunami II

Stood at the door of
His ramshackle hut
In Penang, I knocked.
My family huddled
On the steps, cameras
Raring. This fishing village
Had been knocked hard
But not swallowed. Without
Question, he let us in, dark,
Bespectacled, children
Hanging at his side, wife watching
From a kitchen doorway.
Two rooms in total, crude wood
Floors, one sofa, a few pots. All
Sunk, a month earlier, beneath
Shelves of water, whose mark still
Stains the walls. And on the wall
A single poster – of the tsunami –
Pictures of grief, a woman
Enveloping her dead boy, the
White waves approaching, the
Aftermath of terror and debris.
This was their story. He told
His story, as his children went
To buy expensive seven-ups
For us, who had just knocked.
Hearing I liked the poster
He scraped it off the wall and
Rolled it into my possession:
The story of his story, now
On my suburban wall, which I
Show to those who knock.

PART II

ON BEING A MUSLIM

Muslim Manifesto

To be Muslim, we must believe
In the One God, His prophets, His last Prophet.
We must pray, feed the poor, fast,
And make sacred our pilgrimage.

But this is not all.
We must be clean, at all times,
As when we come before our God.
We must be modest in dress, both
Woman and man.
We must speak gently, not too loud,
Nor walk proudly upon this earth
For one day we will meet our God.
This is the Prophet's example.

We must care for our parents, and
Families; we must love our spouse, be true
To her or him, and bring up our children
In tender knowing of right and wrong.

But this is not all:
We must be honest in all our dealings:
Of business or home or work:
With Muslims and non-Muslims.

It is not enough to pray and fast
And read the Holy Book; this is
Not all the Prophet taught; though he
Spent his night cloaked in prayer, in
His day, he changed the world.

So this is not all; we
Must also do good works,
Seek knowledge, teach, change,
Change the small
Part that is our world.
We must care for our communities:

For their welfare, their health
And cleanliness; we must strive to
Be upright, aim high in all things,
Most of all in giving.

Revelation must come
Just as it came to him. We
Must struggle and strive
And learn the patience of
His vision. To find God,
We must seek the ends of self.

No matter what people say or do
We must act kindly, act with patience,
Our words must bring a smile,
Our bearing must be gentle.

If we practise Islam, we
Will eat and drink
In moderation. Bowing
In prayer will keep us humble,
Even supple; our fasting
Will purify us inside.
Our charity will make us
Strong. Our pilgrimage (all
Life long) will bring us
Peace.

And all of this will
Make you smile, will
Bring release from the
Long day's toil and
 Night's care, will
Make you sweet
In His image.

And one last thing: if we
Truly believe, we must
Know: He knows: there
Is no hiding, no deceiving, He knows

Our deepest motive, our
Most hidden thought. His gaze
Holds not only time and space
But all the depth behind
Your face.

So outer faith is not enough:
We must be pure inside:
Our deepest heart
Must pulse with love
For our Creator, and
His creatures: this
Is the longest, hardest
Pilgrimage:

The soul's journey
To itself. Through sin, through
The darkness, endless depth, over
Sea and desert sand,
Footsteps of archangel,
Voice of God to man.

Our only faith
Is the faith that fills
Our words and actions
In the love of sister, brother.
Our only light
Is the Light of God.
No other.

Partition

You who build partitions
In your mosques, between
Men and women, between
Sunni and Shia, between
Pakistani and Arab, beware
Of daring beyond your
Knowledge, beyond the Prophet's
Example. Do not lay
Your retarded vision at
The feet of scripture, or
Divine law. Do not impose
Your ignorant will on
Your people, your brothers
And sisters. First, lower your
Gaze to see your own depths,
Your own hypocrisy, impurity,
You cannot deceive the God
Whose name is always on your lips,
Who knows your inmost motive,
Your own ego, burning for
Recognition, acclaim. Learn
Before you preach, or the flames
Of hell will teach you how
To teach. And you who build
Partitions between yourselves
And those you oppress, beware.
Your high walls will fall, fall
Upon you, wailing.

Prayer

Ibn al-Arabi, what did you
See in those like me, who pray
As if there were no way, who say
Promises only to themselves.

Each clause on human lips
Must find its answer, its echo,
In divine pause, before moving on, in
Words not quite here nor there:

Prayer is dialogue, contract,
Compact between two worlds;
If thought will not rise, stays here,
All promise is broken.

I pray in secret, concealing my
Soul, remembering the verses
Of Isa as I pray. But

Inner thought rises, sways, begins
To lead astray, as my body tires,
Focus expires, wilting toward sin.

Beneath my prayer for light, for
Guidance and love, spin other
Desires, requests: let my

Tax return be large, let my children
Excel at school, let my family stay
In health; I want everyone to
Do well, but please focus on me,

Let the universe, with all its laws
And universal order, somehow, favor
Me. This is our curse, the rising thought
From below, that will not rise.

Vacancy

Piety clothes him as he rests his forehead
On the rug, in the deepest phase of prayer.
Since he was small, he was bowed in worship,
Not knowing what his words meant, or who was there.

And after all, they are not his words, passed
Down from ancient lines, family commands.
The moment of union, the focused love,
Drilled by submission, into vacant form.

There is a vacancy in his grey soul,
Greyer than the beard, which marks his faith.
What one says no longer matters, mere rites
Through which we lose a right to speak.

It no longer matters, to him, if words
Which house ancient souls, ancient schools of law,
The thought of endless scholars and preachers,
Glide over his life, his deeds, like mist, like breeze.

Untouched, no word ever comes from his soul,
No thought to add to the old body of thought;
Just silence, as he breathes in, breathes out,
In rhyme, words that lived in another time.

And who will judge him if in his silence
He should mock the very Word he should love;
If, bound in the endless words of others,
His tongue cannot strive for the Word above.

The vacancy he has grown to live with,
Will die with: and the deeper emptiness,
The deadened fear that there is nothing, here or there,
Beneath words, rite, ritual prayer, silence, night.

Friday Sermon

As I walk to the side door, men's entrance,
I hear already the screaming, the noise,
Of high-pitched verve, far from the prophet's poise;
I pass through people, smile, inward in stance

As I sit behind the rows of devout
Friends and strangers, half anticipating,
Craving, some small revelation, aching
For guidance as I hear the imam shout

Harsh warnings of Hell, long heard in the West
Until the last centuries, frightening schoolboys,
Such as we have become, fleeing all choice,
Easing only the symptoms of our unrest,

Needing a solace of self-punishment,
A secure bliss of self-imprisonment.

I leave by the same door, not sure at all;
My problems, my inner strivings, remain;
The young man's words can only ever fall
Behind me, dying, in an old refrain.

I wish I were in another world, where
This sermon were given with gentle voice,
Speaking, without script, guiding through hard choice,
Through this-worldliness. How I have longed to hear

Words of the prophet, flowing, forgiving,
Words that will give me sight in the darkness:
Words that help me strive, instead of fleeing,
Words that will hear me when I kneel to confess.

Weight

What is this weight, O Lord, in the heart's core:
Why is your servant still unsure?
How deep can breath reach before it feels You
How vast an expanse must the eye view?

What is this weight in others too, which sinks
Through me so deep it always drinks
Away my faith, my cup, which brimmed with love
Whose thirst awakes but will not move.

What is it speaks in us, veiled syllables,
Beneath our reciting, our parables,
The empire of self struggling from within:
To unchain its rule, regain sin.

Our feet are heavy, stubborn, like the heart,
So lighten the path, ease our part,
So, stumbling, looking back, we always see
Ahead, in time, eternity.

Phantom Ship
(A Lament for Islamic Knowledge)

What treasure lay in her stores:
Volumes, limned with gold and red,
Farabi, Ghazali, frayed scrolls of old
Wisdom, Ibn Hazm, papyrus weighed yellow
Under age, and majesty of algebra, gilt-edged
In symbols; poetry pristine in slim
Calligraphy, philosophy embossed,
Circling out on golden page
Of Medieval gloss; astronomy, the
Heavens laid out in Arabic, myth,
Apothegm. What intellect, apostasy,
Weighed down her sails.

Where did she go? Sailing
From the Eastern sun, on
Reddening seas, ploughing
Shadow of silver-grey, her journey
Just begun, when dark
Lightning struck her sail:
A thousand years
Ago, gazing upon
Al-Ash'ari's face, she
Fled beneath the waves.

Forgotten, betrayed,
Her beams rotting, she
Dreams, from her depth,
Dreams of the
White surface.

Hijab

It is all hidden, I know.
But it is not what you
Show to the world that
Shows you. It is the way
You show, the way you
Don't quite hide beneath
Your scarf, your veil, a hair
Askew, hanging loose, as if
By accident or some hurried
Task or movement. And what
About those painted nails,
Both hands and feet, sometimes
Red and once dark green. And bangles
Too, and small gold anklets, as if
You were some fairy princess
About to dance, in some glass
Realm, where your nimble form
Could roam free. I won't even
Talk of your lips, darkly rouged,
Perfectly poised, as if expecting
To open for some mythic visitor.
More thought, much more, went into
The tiny parts you are allowed to
Show than to those
You are obliged to hide.

New Generation

We're always complaining:
The Jews are so much better,
Cleverer, higher-aiming
Than us, more organized,
More unified. Why can't we
(Who outnumber them
A hundred to one) ever
Get our act together? Let's see:
The Whitefield Jewish youth
Have Cubs, Scouts, Karate
Drama, cookery, computing.
From the Fort Wayne Federation
They attend Jewish Youth
Conventions, arrange trips to Israel,
Liaise with agencies like United Way.
In the Poconos, young Jews have a summer
Camp, abrim with fun and learning.
At Brandeis, an artistic institute
For talented kids from school.
At St. Louis Jewish Center, a big gym
In which all ages can keep trim and fit.
And what do our youth do, our
Local Muslim youth? They
Wonder where to seat their
Women, so their senses
Won't be hit. They sit
About, talking, talking
About where to sit.

To a Secular Cynic

You think you are modern,
Tolerant, humane, enlightened
Beyond the benighted reign
Of other-worldly groping
After false hope or certainty.
You think you are practical, pragmatic, cool,
Scientific, true heir of Enlightenment, breathing
Only rational air.

But your modernity is old, foretold, foregone
In Aquinas and John Donne, Ibn Sina and Ibn
Rushd, al-Ghazali and many more; your
Tolerance ends sharply at the blade of difference, a
Name for fear of all but conformity.
You think you think for your
Self but you have no
Idea where your ideas were made; your
Pragmatism a code (Dante knew) for expedience,
Convenience, and absence of value. You believe
Nothing, and your morals – if any – come
From the dark night from which you think you have
Emerged. The sun in whose
Dazzling you drown yourself
Is the bland light of indifference, of ignorance.
Your humanity, your science rest on
Blind, abstract, dutiful
Devotion.

PART III

LOVE?

Marriage

Don't go from one prison to another:
Your years of girlhood yoked to will of man,
Iron rule of father and then brother:
You dream of escaping your entire clan.

But look behind: your clan reaches long years
Back. And wider than even you can dream.
And can you look ahead, past all your fears
To where their fingers really reach? What seem

To be your ideas are theirs. They'll grip your
Heart from down below: the young man to whom
You run will prove old, with each daily chore,
Enslaving you again. There'll be no room

For who you think you are, even in
Your own room, the one you reserve for sin.

To a Muslim Girl

Lady, lost, in the distant light,
Who are you?
Your veil has covered my face:
Where am I?

I watch my image in your eye:
Who am I?
You are too close for my touch:
Why?

Words fade upon your distant breath,
Cold and lonelier than desire;
You glide from night, untouched by eyes:
You rise like fire, through a dream.

Lady, voiced from a long dark note
In the mind's mist:
Your lips have lost the veil
Which should be kissed.

I watch a shadow by the lake
It is not you or I.
Lady, shivering on cold white ground,
Have you still
The world within your eye.

Muslim Love

You think Muslims
Are repressed, that
They berate love,
That they envy you!
Let's just say: they
Have great love:
If only you knew!

Love in Islam
Is not forbidden, nor
Frowned upon,
Just veiled: like all
Real passion, no need
To flaunt and shout
From moonlit roofs.

Love in Islam
Is tenderness, communion,
Between wife and man: whose
Union, the Prophet said,
(In authentic narrative)
The very deed,
Is charity.

So when you see those
Pretty women in their veils:
Don't pity them, don't
Condescend, or pretend
You know them; they know
Themselves, inside, out.

They know, not just
Love's pleasure, but
Love's just measure,
Its need for trust, its need
To know its station,
To seek its own face.

Love is infinite,
A blessing: so stop viewing
It as transgressing; the Creator
Knew (more than you)
What He was doing.

Honorable Death

Well, we succeeded in
Deceiving the devil. We did
The right thing, avoided evil.
Though we were attracted,
We never yielded to deeds
Of darkness. And now, old,
Our looks all gone, we can
Boldly reflect, retrospect
On our virtue, veritable,
That sliced away at passion,
Piercing all its veins, drowning
It in its own blood; how good
We were, how we squeezed
Its sinful promptings out of breath,
And now we can wait through
Long remaining years, wait
At the gates of honorable death.

Lot of Sin

I live, crouched, at the corners of the world,
The edge of the universe, its quiet limit, where
None can see me. I hide from the stern face of law
And the sharp tongues of human judgment.

My sin is me. I am my sin.

What law demands,
I did not give. I would change
Myself if I could live as something else.
But I am here. With my desire, which
Does not die with threat of fire or
The icy stare of those who guard
The gates of faith with their hate.

In God's wide nature, there is
Room for murderers, thieves,
Torturers, adulterers: all these,
If they relent, repent,
Can receive His grace
And be
Forgiven.

Is my sin greater than these?

They will stone me and kill me,
Throw me from high walls, burn me;
They will curse me even after
My life is done: eternal
Perdition; yet what harm
Have I ever done, to man or woman
Or God's creatures?

They will stone me, who do not
Know me.
I have never said words of hurt;

I have smiled at all who pass;
I have always fasted, prayed
With the poor, with my knees
On dirt floors, shared my flask,
And circled seven times the great shrine.

Give me strength
Not to be, to be free of my
Lot of sin, the sin of being.

But they cannot hear me; my voice
Comes from too far, the quiet limit of
Their universe, too weak for their hearing:
Echoing, eternally in exile, circling,
It comes back to me.

But perhaps, in some corner of God's
Tender infinity, there lies a drop of

Mercy, for me.

Paradise

Who let fall that paradise, to know right
From wrong, let slip the kiss, eternal bliss,
Like a windswept scarf, fallen, from the neck
Of an ancient saint: who scorned the night
Of eternal joy, turning toward the flood,
To feel in veins the thrill, the taste, the haste
Of knowing, moving, disordering within,
The soul sinking itself beneath death,
Into new worlds, of body, skin, touch and sin:
Knowledge born of taint, disobedience:
Woman and man newly aglow in sense,
In worlds without sense, where wisdom is
Pain, and virtue known only when lost
Like a kiss remembered in loneliness.

To Yasmeen, after Nine Years

The years have not dared to
Touch your Beauty
Which sings in the music of eternal spheres;
In you, all is harmony, radiance, wholeness;
In you, Being knows its end, its first and final cause:
There are no edges, no shadows, no burden of excess,
Your stillness moves and your motion stills.

Who am I who could love you?
Who could outform space and time,
Outsense intuition,
Outreach the infinities of Reason?

The vast cycles will move without my words;
The ancient mysteries still sing,
Your voice flowing in their silent notes:
The universal poem
Which Love, not I, can sing.

Ode to Yasmeen

In the saint's garden grew
The vine of jasmine, her
White petals loved
By mystic watering hands, her
Bending, reaching to the mango blossom
Is a spell, binding myth
And human world: vine of jasmine,
Lonely only metaphor, for you alone
Exists the garden, the mystery of the
Holy one's rites, sacrifice, self
Abasement. What action moves to you as fruit
Is drowned in motive, stained in profit
Yet are you human as the world
In your everlasting marriage, the mango blossom's
Cycle of world
Worldless desire, your garden-filled soul.

To My Son Hishaam,
In Karate Class

That eye you show me, as we stretch upon the floor,
Our secret gaze to each other;
I see myself in your eye,
Wrapped in the deepest love I have ever known
A love you never reflect upon
Or speak,
Love which shines, dazzling,
From your deepest eyes.

To My Son Hasan, Sleeping

Lying, oblivious to all
But your dream, you
Don't see the difference
You bring to my eyes
The difference you cast
Through my waking
You affirm
That in the world
I am, that
World too in me.

Repression

I am weighed down
Under centuries of
Prohibition, religion,
Repression; I abide by
The laws, I lower my gaze,
And inwardly frown.
I tell myself you
Are nothing
To me, that you are self
Centered, foolish, immature.
I hold down my desire until it
Drowns. I pound and
Pummel your image
Into the ground. But when
I see you, speak to
You, my breath fails,
And my heart pounds,
Weighed down.

For You (Yes, You)

May the world's harshness pass you by
And your radiance never darken;
May the loneliness of us all never touch you,
And your sweetness never fall
From you;
May your soul flower through your years,
And your years flow smoothly above the rocks;
May your dreams sustain you and raise you high,
Your goodness strengthen you, your aims
Shine before you, in clear streams.
May Night never kiss you with its shadows
And sunlight ever kiss your eyes.
May your children follow you
In loveliness;
And may the God whose beauty you always sing
Always answer you.

Mother

One day you will not be there, sitting
On your armchair, cutting coriander, as I sit
On the sofa with my laptop, typing
And not talking. One day I will need you
To forgive my silences and inattention,
To be there to make tea for, to massage your
Swollen leg, to run to pick up your phone.

I am sorry for all my absences, all the times
I should have been there, when you were
In pain, or returned from hospital, or needed
Groceries. Caught up in the cares of
World and career, e-mails and promotions and
Bank statements. Do not let your absence
Fall upon mine just yet: let me let you
See what you have been to me, what you are
And always will be.

A Letter to my Father

It is twenty years since
My tears fell on your grave. As I near
The age when the earth took you back,
I recall that no human being ever wept
Tears for me like yours; knowing that
You must die and I must leave for another shore,
You cried like a child, uncontrollably, as I
Vanished in the airport, leaving you
With no son.

I have loved and not loved you, as I did
When your laughter sang on earth,
When your handsome face, your laughing charm
Drew friends by the hundred. I was always
Envious of you, your
Ease with humanity, with
Aristocrats, businessmen, poets,
Even the English working class.
Even now, from a past
Bedroom window, I see
You crouched on the grass, smoking
Your pipe, chatting to local workmen,
Laughing, relaxed, as if you
Had no accent.

And I never knew what it was
That made you roll into laughter,
Even in the highest places.
When I was nervous, wondering how
Words could ever come to me,
Even now I wonder what you said
To bring such mirth to strange faces.

After you left, I felt you beside me:
Whenever life blessed me with small success,
I would turn to you, weighed down with
Need of approval, rehearsing
A compulsion nursed since childhood.

As I near your age, I hear your voice in mine,
I see you in the curve of my son's neck,
In my impatience and pride, my anger,
All already passed on to my children.
Everywhere about me you are there.
When I lecture my children, when I
Fail to impress my wife, when I laugh
When students read out their work,
Pronouncing Yeats as if it rhymed with Keats.

But in all that lecturing, in all that
Spurring on, in all the pointing out
That life is an art, that talking with
People is an art, that one's heart
Should be pure; in all of this,
I wonder if I ever heard the voice of love.

I wonder now if my children, my wife
Hear that tiny voice echoing through the
Deepening layers of ancestry, which
Wrap about me from within, so I can
Not know which is me and which is you.

I know that voice was there in
Everything you did for me. It
May just be that I am hard
Of hearing and could not hear
It through the din of voices
That was my world.

But we cannot change our ends.
What chance of beginnings?
Of beginning again? Were we friends,
I would suggest that we begin again,
Forgive each other fully.
But our endings have already begun
And our beginnings ended.

I wonder, if you saw me now,
Whether your pride would be at ease.
Whether your advice would cease:
Higher still and higher. I have not
Reached those heights. But I am
In a higher place, where height
Is not all, and love is.

I will meet you again; if not
In any afterlife, in this one, in the
Selves you bore in me, breathing all
Around me, through people and things:
You have not gone. And we will
Break bread together, our eyes warm,
Healing a lifetime of wounds, we will
Greet the lost years smiling,
Feeling the distant deep of cloud and sun
Touched with love.

Sealed Book
(To a Muslim Girl Seeking Marriage)

If half of life is now a sealed
Book to you, will it open
When, as wife, you
Try to steal pleasures
That, late revealed, we
Monks cannot
Freely give.

Your face is only half-formed;
The face within will take time
To rise to meet your mirror.
Can you feel her
Throbbing? There is
A visage rising deep within, who
Will surprise you. She will
Frown on her estate, she will
Pound against the prison walls;
The beauty of her eyes will burn
Redder than the fires which burn
Books; she will not care for the
Dead smile of any mirror.

The convent walls are high
But she will climb, slipping,
Tearing her toes, nails
Bleeding against rock; again
And again, through years
She will bruise herself, till she
Finds herself at the top:
Between her and
Freedom...
One fearsome fall...

A Muslim Man to a Woman

I don't want you falling
In love with me;
I don't want you looking
In my eyes, expecting surprise at
Your beauty. I don't want to
Hear your marriage is not
Working, how bored you are
With your husband or fiancé, how
Badly he treats you, misunderstands
You, how you
Yearn for passion.

Do not bring this to me: I want
 To know you as a human
Being; I want to converse
With your mind. I don't want
To see your neck or your legs
Or your waist. Or even your painted
Fingernails. I don't want to
Dream of your lips or your hair.
Let me lower my gaze, and let me
See the soul that lives inside you.

Childhood Sweetheart
(To celebrate the wedding of Michael Fitter and Mary)

Many many years ago, before
Memory set in,
We were childhood sweethearts,
And then Life came between us;
Life, with a wife I loved, and two
Darling children, a diamond daughter
And a son, whose socialist intent
Was as stubborn as his sartorial bent;
But I loved and cherished them both.

Now they have all gone.
My dear wife waits under the earth.
My daughter, a mother, my
Son, a father and husband:
All deep in their own lives.

And now, God
In his mystery, in his always
Ineffable Glory, has
Brought you to me
Again. He has
Taken us back through misty years
When memory was love:
Love, which makes our eyes
Young again.

Part IV

Ghazals, Sonnets and Rubaiyat

Ghazal I

I waited for you across long seas; some trace
I sought, of your will in forming the world's face.

I sought you in the love of lovers, but they
Had turned away from memory of your grace.

I sought you in the things of nature, but they
Competed in cruelty, mindless of their place.

I sought you in the smiles of friends, but they
Competed with me, age stiffening their pace.

I sought you in enduring love of family,
In ties of blood, in the firm moorings of race.

I sought you in me, emptying in your embrace.
Nowhere, nowhere is where I found your face.

Avenues

Wide are the avenues leading to hell,
On which we stroll, laughing to each other,
Each clasping his wares, unwilling to sell
His dreams of now for sake of another

World, no matter what we say we believe.
If we truly believed that God was there
We would sell all we had, without reprieve,
And give all to the poor, without a care.

But we live like kings as poor children die,
We turn away from grief except in prayer;
Our charity is for us, to stay high
Above the reach of conscience, betrayer

Of our peace. We love our heaven here so well,
We scarcely see it as the slope of Hell.

Far

I will in silence hold you to my heart,
You whose face will forever be held far;
I will seek you within myself: you are
Always there, from where I must always part.

I know you, lost in silence, are broken:
Reconciled with worlds of loss, without love;
Love between us can never be spoken,
No release for us, below or above.

Let us then in silence lay down our dream;
Let us forget we knew one another;
No other life will lift us from this life's scheme,
Love has gone from us: we are its Other.

Let our paths diverge, as if wrought by art:
Let us in silence wrest love from our heart.

Flood

Looking far, to the edges of his world,
He saw himself beneath the black water.

He saw the will most high, to be unfurled
Before his people: universal slaughter.

Floodgates from on high, black lightning hurled
Purgation on earth's breast, impure daughter.

Inside the ship, they crouch together, curled
In terror, as planks strain, ever tauter.

And we, unchosen to board, to be whirled
Under, watching our short time grow shorter.

Is this the justice which smashes the world:
Crashing with thunder of high laughter.

Rubaiyat
(On the marriage of Vaseema and Luis)

Who dreamed of purple Caesars, empires gone;
The ruined treasures of Ctesiphon;
Persian versions of our past in verse and song;
Fountained avenues of Bukhara, which shone.

Who dreamed that the fountain and the rose;
The nightingale, couch, and night of love's throes;
Who dreamed that these long drowsing pasts
Could wake into song? What fate dreams, who knows?

Who dreamed that dreams could bring your waking smile,
Bearer of sunrise, to my long trial;
From beneath ruins and sleeping columns,
Unwritten in me, in my long exile.

Who dreamed your eyes: bearers of silent streams,
Still music, beneath the noise of what seems;
Mirrors of treasure, hidden until now,
Bringing me to love, love deeper than dreams.

Ghazal II
(For Yasmeen)

It is the language of poets and of kings
Which awakens on your breath, speaking things

Unheard in my world, unsung in verse or rhyme:
I hear from afar the whispered longings

Of an ancient time: Bukhara, Samarqand,
Voices waking now in the voice that rings

In my dreaming ears. I am now waking
To my own past, to the music that brings

Your smile to my dreaming eyes. Our love sings
In self-knowing, soaring on ancient wings.

Ghazal III
(Translated from the Urdu of Siddiqua Shabnam)

Far, far from red flowers, and roses blushing near,
Far, far from jasmine and stalk, lush in green each year;

Far, far from your garden is our journey;
We are fated forever to go from here.

Far, far must I stay from my land, my home:
Each morning falls on me like night's blackness here.

Far, far from the soil of Deccan, my lost earth,
Spring falls like the dying of Autumn here.

Stylish Shabnam has found a new voice to wear:
Far, far from the voices long past, yet near.

Part V

Political Musing

To a Suicide Bomber

You do not speak for me:
You who soak yourselves in blood
Are far from the Prophet's mantle.

You who act beyond the Book
Are far from the Word.

You do not speak for me:
You who do not know, and kill,
Murder your own soul.

You blew up a young girl.
A mother's heart will bleed forever.
A father's will is broken.
Because of you their world is ended.

What good have you done?

Your own wife, young,
Curses you in her sleep, her nightmare.
Your children betrayed
To a myth; they do not know where you are,
Where you have gone; they still ask for you.
Your parents dragged
Through your empty dream.
Because of you their world is ended.
You have brought not paradise
But hell: hell to all around you.
Their ghosts will rise around you,
Asking: Why? Why?

What good have you done?

Because of you, I am reviled;
Because of you, your own people suffer;
Because of you
Oppression speaks louder.
Because of you, my religion reels in shame.

Because of you, two countries lie in ruins.
Because of you, a deserted nation suffers.
Because of you, the corrupt have grown stronger.
The bigots can speak without shame.
Because of you, the good people the world over
Have no name.

With each act of your violence,
Your enemies grow stronger, harsher
More justified in killing and conquest.
Each life you take weakens your cause, turns
An indifferent world against you.

You call yourselves holy warriors:
But you have never read the Holy Book
Never tried to understand
Never struggled with yourself.
You took the easy way:
And what will you say on the Day of Days?
What will you say to your Lord, to
Those you killed, to your family?
What good have you done?

It is not you who bear
The Prophet's sword; the
True sword is a word, a thought,
Touched by light, forged
In wisdom and
Relentless in love.

It is not you who wear
The Prophet's mantle but those who
Strive, armed not with bombs but with
Patience, with a Book,
High in words and deeds.

You do not speak for me
Or the sweetness of my God;

You do not speak for me.

Suicide

He lies on his bed, dreaming:
Young boy, with no sleep
In his head, no toys in his hand,
And dusty feet.
When will my paradise come?

The dusty street holds no promise.
Everywhere lie ruins: his school,
One room, bombed. Three small girls
Burned instantly to death, sat
With alphabet in hand. Half a wall
Remains, mud, a few papers in the dust:
There was little before. Now, less
Than nothing.

His aunt's apartment was blown
Open to the winds, human
Habitation shook back to earth, tremors
Shaking your heart.
His cousin Ali from his tiny coffin
Still speaks to him, still jokes
About Lubna and her long nose;
Aisha, once twirling, like a little dervish,
Her scarf, opening like a sail
To the winds, lies next to him,
Her coffin smaller.

When will my paradise come?

He sees them. Soldiers,
Barricading human traffic, hours
Of waste, leering, scowling, hours
To kill, arrogance of
Power. Such were Roman soldiers
In this very land, and Greeks, and Persians,
And what of Germans. His life has been lived

Many times before. Endless children
Have squatted, helpless, witness
As fathers were forced to bow, mothers
To open their wombs
To seeds of violence.

His mother scolds, runs
Her fingers through his hair,
I need bread, get off your bed
And do something
For once. Head on his hands,
Lying, he can see the sky,
Lose himself in shapes,
Drifting always away.

His father's grave
Has no mound, just crude
Markings on an earth that
Forgets without forgiving.
His smile, stained teeth, crushed
With a rifle's butt, are
Gone. His voice grows fainter, every day,
Drifting always away.

To remember is the struggle:
This hell was not always;
Even in exile, there were smiles,
Family, men sharing cigarettes,
And women, secrets; huddled around
Hookahs, coffee, smoke,
Tent curtain flapping.

And before that, who knows?
What rivers flowed, what boughs overhung
What date palms grew, and olives,
What myths, what biblical promises. Did we
Ever have a home?

When will my paradise come?

Now, even memory lies in ruins.
Our pasts have deserted us.
Our present bows its head.
Our future, over the hills, is
Taken daily, plot by plot.
Our leaders are useless.
Our time is gone, long gone,
All drifted away.

There is nothing left in me.
Nothing to destroy.
All drifted away.
I am dead.

My paradise: I will come.

A Poem for Neda
(Shot by the Iranian militia during elections in Iran)

Neda.

Sweet voice,
Of freedom, unborn.

Your state totters.
A color revolution.

Green, for life,
Of reason, faith;
Red for the blood
You lost, unpaid.

And you have betrayed
Your color, you
Whose voices rise
Above your people
Who cast your black sky
Over all voices;
Who hide behind
Arms and words;
Who cringe
Behind your flag.

Tears will find you out.

And you too, betray
Your color, who
Watch from afar,
In fear, who flirt
With freedom's name;
Who smile unashamed
As tyrants old or new
Play your cards for you.

Tears will blind your smiles.

You who love
Your daughters, sons,
Let the green of earth be
Your color:
Let your love give birth
To the Islam which your poets dreamed.

Let your voice, which sang
Before, of golden Persia,
In Saadi, Hafez, Rumi,
Now return, to sing
Our future.

Let your sweet voice
Sing from the cold earth
Of sweet democracy
Buried in its birth.
Dreaming to be
Born.

Daughter, sweet voice
Of the new Iran:
Neda.

A Prayer for Gaza

I am Gaza.
I am the poem of Gaza.
The world does not see me:
A world which does
Nothing.

You launchers of rockets, I ask you now:
Lay down your arms, your useless arms:
See what gifts from the enemy they bring:

They rain down terror from the air;
They burn our children's faces;
They turn our schools to rubble;
They churn our homes to dust.
And the world does nothing.

So I beg you now, you launchers of rockets,
Lay down your arms: what have they brought in
Fifty years? Nothing.
Your killing of civilians
Can bring nothing
But shame. In taking
Such life, your blame
Will burn in the eyes of God.

The powers we face are incalculable. We
Cannot win by arms. We cannot even
Win with words; the powers we face
Are endless in resource; they control
What is known and what is not known.

They control a world of words
Which does nothing.

You launchers of rockets, you surely know:
They will answer your terror with their terror:
They will take more lives in ten days
Than you can take in ten years.
They will blacken your skies.

They will rain down terror from the air;
They will burn our children's faces;
They will turn our schools to rubble;
They will churn our homes to dust.
And the world will do nothing.

Lay down your rockets, your home-made guns:
Or they will take more
And more of our land. They
Will not be merciful: their soldiers laugh as
Our women are slaughtered; their settlers
Take our villages and farms;
These are not the true children,
These are not the true Jews:
Who taunt our children
Who thirst in endless queues.
While the world does nothing.

Lay down your guns, your tired rockets.
They will not be merciful; so you must
Show mercy. I do not ask you to forget,
Forget the suffering, still bleeding
Through our people. I ask that
You think of your children;
Of all children.

Let our enemy know that we will not
Strike again. Though his weapons are
Fearsome, he himself is full of fear;
Though his arms are strong, he himself is weak.
He has a nuclear power beyond our
Dreams, but still he lives in fear.
He needs to know.

He has imprisoned us
Imprisoned himself
Within a wall: the symbol of his fear.
He needs to know.

Let us sit down with our enemy.
Talk with him as though
He were our friend.
(One day we must remember: the Jews
Are our brothers, descended
From the same father Abraham.
The Jews are not our enemy, no
Matter what deeds
Go forth in their name; the
True Jews of the world are friends; they
Bleed with you, ashamed
Of those who pretend to their name,
One day we must live with them as friends.)

Let us use a courage higher than your rockets,
Stronger than his tanks:
Let us tear down this wall; and all walls between us.
Let us sit down, and talk. And let us spread
This message through our people: no more
Violence, no more talk of wiping out
The enemy. It is not just violent acts which bring
His violent retribution, but violent words.
Let him know that he is safe.
The greatest courage is to know
One day we must live as friends.

I am Gaza, the poem of Gaza.
I am Muslim, Christian, Palestinian and Jew.
I am you.

A Prayer for Zia Rahman
(Who built a Mosque in Voorhees, with the kind help of Jews, Christians and Buddhists)

Your journey was hardly begun:
Now faded into deep starlight, gone
From this night.

Amid shouting and noise,
Amid screaming, you kept
Your poise, spoke always with
Gentle voice, even to those
Who stood loudly
Opposed.

And now, you have left
Your silence with us,
Your gentle pleading.
Your smile is still with us,
Your dream still needing
Our love.

And you have left,
On earth, the lovely symbol
Of your dream, of the power
Of Faiths when they
Dream together

Salam, shalom, peace
Be upon you, friend of all.
May He in Whose
Infinite call
Our journey begins and ends
Bring you to grace, to gardens
Where rivers flow beneath your feet,
May He make your journey sweet.

Knife

Little girl,
Where did you go?
When did your world,
Your little laugh,
Stop?

You hardly had time
To grow, skipping
With playmates, on
Your slow way to school.

You were born
In your body, you
Did not choose; nor
Did your Creator
Refuse your joy.

And then night fell.
The knife fell. Centuries
Of darkness fell on
You.

They held you, screaming,
Knees apart:
Your loving aunts, all
Uncomprehending,
Cutting, cutting,
Your mother's sadness
Silent, unbending.

And now, you cannot
Love: man, woman, God.
They have torn out
Your little soul.

And they, who sanction
This, mullahs and tribesmen
Who know not what they do:
Will they answer
For the life they tore?

Little girl,
In some other world,
Will you laugh?
As before?

Doors

I hear them creaking
The doors of ijtihad,
Unoiled, through centuries, soiled
With rust and grime, I hear them
Creaking in lonely minds spread far apart
In space and time, longing to meet
Where and when they might
Greet each other's open worlds.

They whisper through the centuries:
The voice of the thief, face bruised,
Who waits in his heart for the words
Of the Prophet, gentle, forgiving,
Understanding his weakness, as his
Earthly judges stand before him
Commanding the blade that will sever
Forever the very veins and nerves
His creator put together.

They whisper from far-off places:
An African girl, asking why,
Why must they take the blade to me,
Don't let her cut me; the mother's
Softness hardened by blindness
And memory of her own bleeding
Between legs held apart
By smothering aunts.

They whisper in the voice of poets
Whose lives burst open the
Spines of sacred texts; the woman
Sat, with her son, creating her space
In a Karachi apartment, unsafe
From the glares of mullahs and men.

I hear them creaking,
The rusty, grimy doors of ijtihad.
Guarded day and night by
Piles of dead upon dead.
But buried wisdom is waking; its
Birth will break the very earth,
It will uproot these rotting gates
That have locked in so much hate.
It will replace them, displace them
With nothing.

Muslim Slave

I am black, I am woman; native, but
These are words on the tongues of others.
Parched my lips from centuries of work, my
Clothes caked with mud, my black feet brown

With dust. I own no thing. I am owned by many.
My mouth opens for food and sometimes for lust
Of black husband, white master: I am their tool
In the fields, their instrument of self-worth, yet

I do not speak. My inner mouth is closed, sealed
Like ammunition. There are voices.
Voices all around, screaming, preaching
Everywhere. All day long I am thrown

Between master and master, field and sky,
Empty stomach, burned face. No-one looks
Me in my empty eye. Outwardly, I no
Longer feel. But my inner thought peals like

Prayers, vibrating in my soul, sounding
A world so far away it hurts my whole mind.
Yet there, I am: dancing in yellow fields and
Flowers, not far from the gate of the garden.

Language

Brown boy, first day of school
Hears only sounds, which sting
His ears, stifle his tongue,
In the cold, damp day.
His own thoughts play
Under the blaze of
A foreign sun.

They tease, toy, laugh:
Brown boy can't speak,
But he squeals if you
Pinch his dirty skin
Which won't wash off
In the school basin.

Brown boy cannot speak.
His language lies
Buried beneath domes,
Lost years, dim places,
Across long seas and tears
On brown long faces.

Its tongue is choked,
Crushed under crumbled walls of
Ctesiphon, Bukhara, Samarqand.
In the camps of Afghan hordes,
Courts of Delhi, Lucknow,
Decaying Mughal palaces.
What futures hold his words:
Mushairas in London, Chicago,
He does not yet know.

Where is that urchin, brown
As his friends, who owned
The dust on which he ran, crouched,
Played? His story sunk beneath
Layers of dirt, history, like
Some buried city, until
Coaxed into view by brush
And spade and deepening will.

He lies buried
Alive in his words, in the
Tongue that rises to speak
And forgets itself, sneaking
Back into its cave of lost
Words, strange syllables,
Murmuring, beneath
The voice which fills
His foreign mouth, his
Dirty suncracked lips.

Home
(Hanif Kureishi)

I want to go home now, said Anwar,
Rancid, jaded, staring into, through, his
Handsome nephew. Enough. I've had
Enough of this damned place, this
Race which hates us, throws stones
Into our store, even pigs' bones which
They know is against our codes. Speak
To your aunt, persuade her to come
Back, back to Bombay, to life
Without skinheads and grey skies,
Streets which won't scowl, bus
Drivers who don't frown
As we fumble aboard.

Sitting on his bed, blinds drawn,
He drums his dirty fingers
On Karim's knee, looks wistfully
Into eyes looking elsewhere,
Reflects, corrects himself:
But what is the point, my boy? Even
India is foreign now; even this
(Pinching his own body)
Is a strange country, reviling me,
Refusing to recognize me.
This brown skin is flaking, daily,
My hair gone, white, my hands
Tremble at me, my teeth bite me,
The whole thing rising in rebellion,
My tenancy is nearly up:
It wants me out, repatriated, gone
To where I came from.
(Gazing at an empty glass)
I want to go home.
Home.

Return
(to India)

A woman washing her children's clothes
By the rocks of a stream,
Eyes dark, unquestioning:
The mild reflection is her only truth.
Along the shore a young man walked,
Gazing at the nearness of sea and sky,
Dust in his image, a shadow,
Sliding into vast of distance:
He is gone.

Beggar
Growing from childhood,
The desperate competence of early days
Melting into adult shame;
These children who sing for their parents' keep
Blur the face behind the proffered hand.

By the temple's foot, I knelt
Whispering dreams that have spoken
Their shame before into silent minds,
Carving images from unknown stone.

I dream of the dying
Gaze of a Mughal emperor
Toward the black domes he will never see:
More foreign than the postcards
I am here, *hinne-ni.*

On Your Beheading of Your Wife
(To the Founder of a Muslim Television Station)

We were all excited: you
Were building a bridge, a
Pioneering path between
Islam and the West; we were
Anticipating small wonders, miracles
Of communication, dreams of
Harmony. Understanding. Struggling
Against stereotypes. And then, instead
Of displaying the beauty of your faith
You went and cut off your wife's head.

I cannot tell you how many
Dreams you have drowned, plunged
Into deep regression. How many years,
How many centuries you have taken us
Back. To the Crusades, to Dante,
To talk of turning Turk, blood rites,
Exotic women, emotional men,
All irrational. Back through ages dark to
The hollow millennium.

May your judgment come now
And hereafter; may the sweet woman
Whose breath you did not deserve,
Fill your dreams, rise up in
Your nightmares, tug at
Your throat, tormenting;
May her tortured, terrified face show
You what you are.

The World Does Not Hate America

They don't hate us: that's a lie
Spewed by those who dare not travel
And a few who travel but dare not look.

You can go
To the farthest corners
Of our small earth: everywhere, they say
The same thing: "We like you, we like things American
We love your burgers and chicken, your movies truly move us;
We even dress like you now, forgetting our own customs, our
Own past and lovely costumes; we imitate
Your T.V. programs, American Idol, Apprentice, the whole lot.
We want big houses and roads like yours, we want
The American dream. But
Leave us alone; please,
Leave us alone."

"Don't bring your soldiers and your tanks here:
Keep them at home, with their loving families.
We don't want to hear any more planes
Booming in the skies overhead while
We try to sleep; we don't want our schools and our roads
Turned to rubble.
There's a lot wrong with our poor country, yes,
We are not always fond of our rulers, but
We have enough to eat, and a place to live, and
No-one bothers us; everything works,
Slowly, and scrappily, but
It works, and we are happy. We are not like you, we know
But we'll get there, in our own way.
We like you, we really do,
And we love your new President, but
Please, please:
Leave us alone."

They do not hate us. Even now. Let us
Leave them alone.

Let us spend
Our money on ourselves: on schools for our young
Homes for our elderly; education for
Our poor. Let us show
The joys of true freedom, the voice
Of true democracy. Let us
Lead by example of justice and reason. Let us
Be the first to extend the hand of compassion. Then
The world will come to us. Then neither we
Nor the world
Will be alone.

Valentine War

And who will write songs of love for you
When war has scarred all song.
When bombs have burned enough children,
Scorched their cities, disfigured their deserts,
When tyrants have played out their game of oil and empire,
Leaving the earth's fields drenched in blood, the air poisoned,
The atmosphere shaking with terror, prisons echoing with
torture;
When greedy kings of commerce have squeezed their grip
On all the resources of the world;
When the hate-spewing media have drained the human voice
Of all song:
What love is left in me?

What love has left in me I leave for love:
No commerce will it have with the hatred,
The demon, that possesses the vile voice
Of self-anointing leaders. Let their violent words
Pass over us, beneath us, mere noise; our love
Will not yield to their anger, will not see itself
Mirrored in their fuming, bitter, scowling faces.

Let them blacken the green earth, burn up its beauty,
Let them darken the sky with their death-seeking missiles;
They cannot take our world from us; we will be there
When they are finished. We will rebuild what the monsters have
deformed;
Our love will stand when their hatred has spent itself;
And when their voices are silent, hoarse with screaming,
Then we shall write again those songs of love.

Letter to Our Children

Children.
Forgive us.
We have burned the earth.
We have been wasteful.
There is not much left for you,
Much of anything.
We have been aggressive.
Murderous. Mass.
The earth is torn by war.
Nuclear bombs and weapons
Which still poison your soil.
Children starve by the thousand
While we thirst for oil.
And you will starve by the million.
A handful of us are rich beyond measure.
The rest struggle to stay alive.

The world is coming back in
Vengeance: the
Sun burns; the seas rise.
The flood is nearing.
Every religion has shamed itself.
The human has sunk beyond redemption.
We have made your life impossible.
We, your fallen parents.
Can you ever
Forgive us?

To the Muslims of the Twenty-First Century

Sweet children of our future,
Do not follow us:
We are the old generation, tired, disabled, corrupt.
Find your own path.

All we had to do
Was follow the Book. But we
Did not even read it. We recited it
Without knowing what it meant.
We were commanded to read:
But we cannot read.

We were blessed with oil, but we
Bled it into a curse:
We could have created colleges, filled with the
Light of the world's highest learning,
Schools to bring our people forward, returning to
Our glittering past; educating,
Enlightening, financing
Throughout East and West.

But we have built not even one,
Not one renowned college:
All the great scholars are in the West:
Where are our scholars?
Who comes to us to learn
Any science or art? Our colleges are
Beautiful on the outside only; inside
They are prisons of
Dullness, and decay of intellect.

Where are our great philosophers? They are
All in the past: al-Farabi, al-Ghazali,
Ibn Arabi: they are sleeping, and we
Dare not wake them; we
Dare not hear their voices.
We have no great philosophers today, not one:
No great thinkers; our novelists
And poets speak with a
Lonely voice.

We could have forged great alliances;
We could have fostered science and art;
We could have built our own cars, our own
Satellites, our own spaceships;
We could have renewed our great traditions
Of medicine, astronomy, science;
We could have spread Islam's ideal of charity
Through Asia and Africa; we could have
Shown the world a different path, a
World consumed in dark worship
Of capital; we
Could have shown the world
A path of light.

But instead, we plunged into the world's
Darkness; we traded the poetry of our desert heart
For the urban prose of the world; we fostered
Ignorance, backwardness, dependence
On decadence. We built
Luxury hotels and playgrounds for
The playboys of the West,
While our own playboys played in Europe.

But instead, we tried to be like them
Driving luxury cars, wearing
Their clothes, watching their films, listening
To their music, pretending all the time
To the strictest forms of faith, veiling
Our populations in night, in the stubborn
Gloom of a feudal past.

We cared nothing for our people's voices;
Or for the Prophetic past which taught
Consensus, community. Our politics are
Mired in self-seeking blindness: we cannot
See ourselves, cannot think for ourselves:
Mired in tradition, blind imitation,
In the unholy night of unreason.

We financed the narrowest Islam in many nations,
We financed activists, whose actions for half-a-century
Have achieved nothing; less than nothing: we are
Worse than before.

And we have done nothing for
Palestine: its people suffer
Even more oppression,
Even more cruelty
Than before: the
Muslim world lies asleep
Beneath the feet that tramp the world
In search of freedom.

The shapeless feet of Capital.

Sweet children of the future,
You are orphans: your parents are dead,
They left you nothing.
Muslims of the future, beautiful
Dark-eyed men and women, be beautiful
In your words and deeds,

In your clothes and manners, beautiful
In intelligence and love:
Awake from the past centuries' slumber!
Awake, to find your own freedom;
Awake to your true dream.

And do not follow us:
Our dreaming is not over, we cannot wake.
We cannot tell you which path to take:
We do not know.
We have fallen into endless night, the deep forest:
We are lost.

Seek your own path;
Seek the true dawn of Islam, which
We did not find.

Seek the true Light of the One God.

GLOSSARY

Al-Ash'ari	(874-936), influential theologian and founder of the Ash'ari theological school
azan	(Arabic) The call to prayer, traditionally delivered from the minaret of a mosque
dervish	(Arabic, Persian) an ascetic and mystic
Farabi	(c. 878-c. 950), philosopher, considered as second only to Aristotle in the medieval Muslim world
fitna	(Arabic) trial; charm; enticement; intrigue; sedition, dissension, division
Ghazali	(c. 1055-1111), widely influential Sunni jurist, theologian, philosopher and mystic
Hafez	(1315-90), the most celebrated of Persian lyrical poets
hinne-ni	(Hebrew) "Here I am."
Hira	The Prophet's first revelation in the Cave of Hira on the Mountain of Light
hijab	the headscarf traditionally worn by Muslim women; also "curtain" or "cover"
hookah	(Urdu, Hindi) A water pipe used to smoke tobacco
Ibn Arabi	(1165-1240), highly influential mystic and philosopher of Islamic Spain
Ibn Hazm	(994-1064), litterateur, jurist, historian and theologian of Islamic Spain
Ibn Rushd	(1126-98), philosopher of Islamic Spain, who influenced Aquinas. Also known as "Averroes."
Ibn Sina	(979-1037), Persian philosopher and physician. Also known as "Avicenna."

ijtihad	(Arabic) Individual reasoning. There is a saying that by the end of the tenth century, the doors of ijtihad were closed, after which Islamic theology somewhat crystallized.
Isa	Jesus
mushaira	(Urdu) a poetic symposium
Mughals	An imperial Muslim dynasty (r. 1526-1857) that at times ruled most of the Indian sub-continent
Neda	(Neda Agha Soltan, 1982-2009), killed during the Iranian election protests of 2009
Rumi	(1207-73), the great Persian poet and mystic
Saadi	(c. 1213-91), one of the great Persian poets